Pescetarian Diet

Recipe Book/Companion Guide

D0828206

Foreword/Introduction

This book is meant to complement our feature book entitled "Pescetarian Diet: The Ultimate Guide for Understanding Pescetarianism And What You Need to Know".

That book was written to give you all the information you need before starting the Pescetarian diet, which is known for its tremendously positive effect on health and vitality. This book contains recipes that follow the guidelines laid out in that book.

You should fully understand the nuances of this diet before you undergo this new lifestyle. After reading that book, you can use these recipes. If you already have a strong understanding of how this diet can affect your health, then you can begin here.

In this book, you'll find handy Pescetarian food preparation tips and recipes. The recipes are perfect for those who want to slowly migrate to a Pescetarian diet. Aside from some of the oils and condiments used in the recipes, there is hardly any trace of non-seafood animal material in these recipes.

We wish you exciting days ahead with over 50 recipes to choose from in this book!

Happy cooking!

Copyright 2015 by Wade Migan - All rights reserved.

This document is geared towards providing exact and reliable information in regards to the topic and issue covered. The publication is sold with the idea that the publisher is not required to render accounting, officially permitted, or otherwise, qualified services. If advice is necessary, legal or professional, a practiced individual in the profession should be ordered.

In no way is it legal to reproduce, duplicate, or transmit any part of this document in either electronic means or in printed format. Recording of this publication is strictly prohibited and any storage of this document is not allowed unless with written permission from the publisher. All rights reserved.

The information provided herein is stated to be truthful and consistent, in that any liability, in terms of inattention or otherwise, by any usage or abuse of any policies, processes, or directions contained within is the solitary and utter responsibility of the recipient reader. Under no circumstances will any legal responsibility or blame be held against the publisher for any reparation, damages, or monetary loss due to the information herein, either directly or indirectly.

The information herein is offered for informational purposes solely, and is universal as so. The presentation of the information is without contract or any type of guarantee assurance.

The trademarks that are used are without any consent, and the publication of the trademark is without permission or backing by the trademark owner. All trademarks and brands within this book are for clarifying purposes only and are the owned by the owners themselves, not affiliated with this document.

Table of Contents

Chapter 1: Essential Pescetarian Food Preparation Tips

Chapter 2: Salads, Appetizers, And Soups

- Smoked Salmon and Asparagus Roll-Ups

- White Fish Sesame Salad

- Cranberry Tuna Salad

- Asian Scallop Soup

- Seafood Cioppino with Tomato Broth

- Western Shrimp Salad

- Tuna Salad

- Shrimp and Pineapple Skewers

Chapter 3: Salmon And Halibut Recipes

- Whole Poached Salmon

- Dill and Caper Salmon Burgers

- Halibut in Butter Sauce

- Halibut Tacos with Citrus Dressing

- Curry Salmon

- Baked Salmon

- Spicy Salmon Steaks

- Tropical Coconut Salmon

- Poached Halibut

- Salmon Caesar Salad

- Halibut in Lemon Cream

- Broiled Salmon

- Halibut Teriyaki

- Salmon Roe and Cucumber Rounds

- Salmon with Tomatoes and Mushroom

Chapter 4: Tuna, Cod, And Game Fish Recipes

- Coconut Citrus Tuna Steaks

- Baked Cod

- Breakfast Tuna Sashimi

- Grilled Tuna Steaks

- Spicy Coconut Fish

- Cajun Catfish Bake

- Grilled Snapper

- Peruvian Style Picante Mackerel

- New England Baked Fish

- Sweet and Savory Swordfish

- Baked Haddock Italian Style

- Tuna Sailor-Style

- Red Snapper in Zesty Sauce

- Roasted Swordfish with Mushrooms

- Baked Tuna

- Cod with Lemon Dressing

- Baked Trout

- Salt Baked Snapper

- Baked Cod Nuggets

Chapter 5: Shrimp, Crab, Squid, And Shellfish Recipes

- Shrimp Stuffed with Avocados

- Barbecued Alaskan Shrimp

- Shrimp Delight

- Steamed Mussels

- Crab Dip

- Lime and Dill Crab

- Squid with Tomato and Basil

- Broiled Lobster Tail

- Oyster Shooters

- Peach and Ginger Scallops

- Scallops with Almonds and Bacon

Conclusion

Chapter 1:

Essential Pescetarian Food Preparation Tips

Before delving deep into preparing Pescetarian cuisine, here are some practical tips to help make your cooking experiences more rewarding and tasteful.

Seafood handling and safety

Seafood can be tricky. Its shelf life without refrigeration is typically shorter than meats and poultry. Also, it does not hold up well as a leftover, unless it is fried with thick coats of breadcrumbs. Cooked seafood is not as appetizing as roast beef or baked chicken after a week in the refrigerator.

Contamination can also be a problem. Fish breathe air in a different environment than other sources of protein. These environments can be contaminated and fishermen may be unaware of chemicals introduced into their environment. Though it might be a little more expensive, seafood should be bought from reputable outlets. It is also a good idea to find out what area they come from. Seafood should be cleaned and washed thoroughly before preparation in order to minimize contamination.

Unless seafood is consumed in a restaurant, preparation of raw seafood recipes, such as sashimi and sushi, should be left in the hands of capable restaurant personnel. Seafood must be well (not over) cooked for safe consumption.

Ingredients

In keeping with the healthy theme of the Pescetarian diet, recipe ingredients should have the lesast possible amounts of saturated fat, refined sugars, preservatives, and chemical additives. Virgin olive oil and coconut oil should be used instead of other cooking oils containing high levels of unsaturated or "trans fats" present in most vegetable oils.

When adding eggs to a dish, try to stay with eggs from naturally fed hens, or eggs that are infused with Omega-3 oils. Refined sugar should be substituted with natural sweeteners, if possible. Instead of refined table salt, consider using coarse sea salt or sodium reduced salt.

As for condiments, it is always a good choice to go natural, especially for the spices, such as basil, coriander, and dill weed. The alternatives are powdered and/or dried herbs that can be used without sacrificing much of the intended flavor.

Preparation Methods

There will be few recipes here that will involve a little sautéing, but try to avoid frying if at all possible. While frying may appear to be the easiest and safest way to cook seafood, it actually sends most of the nutrients to the un-consumed pool of oil at the bottom of the pan.

Frying also increases the fat content of the dish. When fish is deep-fried in high temperatures, there is also a risk of forming toxic by-products. There are many alternatives for preparing delicious seafood, including baking, poaching, broiling, grilling, and pan roasting. Also, remember that the recommended internal cooking temperature of fish is around 145 degrees.

Substitutions and More Tips to Remember

While the recipes here specify certain fish types, you can substitute some fish types for those specified.

Certain fish types, such as salmon, tuna, and Chilean sea bass, have more fat content than other varieties (typically about 5%). As a result, these types are more flavorful than "lean" fish, such as tilapia, cod or halibut. Once again, remember that more fish fat, to an extent, is good for you because of the Omega-3 oils.

Of course, the leaner fish types have their own strengths. They tend to have a firmer consistency and texture, which makes them the perfect choice for stews, chowders, and soups.

Most fishes can be used interchangeably. However, it is a good idea to talk to your grocer if you plan to substitute seafood types before you cook.

Now, let's cook!

Salads, Appetizers And Soups

Smoked Salmon and Asparagus Roll-Ups

Ingredients

8 ounces wild smoked salmon

12 asparagus spears

12 natural or Omega-3 eggs

1 teaspoon olive oil

½ red onion, thinly sliced

Directions

Slice or snap off the bottom part (about 2-4 inches) of the asparagus spears.

In boiling water, cook the asparagus 3-5 minutes until it is still fairly firm.

Warm a small skillet with olive oil.

Whisk the eggs and pour 2-3 tablespoons of egg in.

Swirl the skillet around while evenly spreading the egg in a very thin layer.

Let cook for around 1 minute until firm, and then slide out it of the pan. Repeat the process until the eggs are gone. This process creates an egg "crepe."

Lay a crepe on a flat surface. On one end, layer some salmon with an asparagus spear and onion slices.

Roll up the filled crepe. Repeat this process with remaining crepes and asparagus spears.

White Fish Sesame Salad

Ingredients

1 pound cod or other white fish

4 tablespoons sesame oil for the salad dressing

3 tablespoons sesame oil for cooking the fish

4 tablespoons mayonnaise

1 tablespoon white or rice vinegar

2 teaspoons sesame seeds, lightly toasted

½ cup finely chopped green onion

Directions

Drizzle the fish with three tablespoons of sesame oil and sprinkle this with salt.

Broil the fish in a high temperature for five minutes per side.

Flake the fish into pieces lightly with a fork.

Place the dish and in the refrigerator.

For the dressing, mix the 4 tablespoons of sesame oil, vinegar and mayonnaise.

Drizzle the mixture over fish.

Add just enough sesame seeds and onions to coat fish.

Cranberry Tuna Salad

Ingredients

12 oz. of canned tuna in water

2 celery stalks, finely chopped

¼ cup red onion, finely chopped

¼ cup low fat or homemade mayonnaise, or more to taste

½ cup dried cranberries

Directions

Simply mix all the ingredients together in a bowl.

Asian Scallop Soup

<u>Ingredients</u>

½ lb. scallops

1 tablespoon butter

1 tablespoon fresh ginger, finely chopped

2 garlic cloves, minced

1 can (about 12 oz.) coconut milk

2 cups chicken stock

1 red bell pepper, cut into thin strips

2 scallions, finely chopped

¼ cup lime juice

¼ cup basil, finely chopped

<u>Directions</u>

Heat the butter in a deep saucepan in medium heat.

Add the ginger and garlic and sauté briefly.

Lightly salt the scallops and add these to the pan.

Sauté the scallops for about 3 minutes, and then add the chicken stock, coconut milk, bell peppers, and scallions.

Bring to a gentle boil, then remove from heat and stir the dish in the lime juice and basil.

Add salt, Tabasco or hot sauce to taste.

Seafood Cioppino with Tomato Broth

Ingredients

1 pound mussels

½ pound clams

1 pound halibut or cod

½ pound scallops

1 white onion, chopped

1 fennel bulb, sliced into thin strips

3 garlic cloves, finely chopped

1 cup cooking wine or dry white wine

2 cups fresh tomatoes, chopped or 1 medium can (about 14 oz.) diced tomatoes in juice

3 cups fish or chicken stock

Salt, pepper to taste

Springs of parsley to garnish

2 tablespoons olive oil

Directions

Mix all the ingredients in a large pot.

Sauté the onion and fennel in a few tablespoons of butter or olive oil until soft, about five minutes.

Add garlic, then wine and bring to a boil.

Add tomatoes and stock. Boil for 10 minutes, stirring occasionally.

Add seafood and stir so that all the seafood is mostly covered by broth.

Cover and cook until the clams and mussels begin to open, or for about 5-6 minutes.

Add salt and pepper to taste and garnish with the parsley.

Western Shrimp Salad

Ingredients

1 lb. cooked bay shrimp, or shrimp.

½ pound cooked crab meat

½ red onion, minced

1 teaspoon paprika

2 teaspoons squeezed lemon juice

1 teaspoon dried dill weed

1 teaspoon freshly squeezed lemon juice

3 cups chopped lettuce, into strips

1 hard-boiled egg, sliced

1 large cucumber, sliced into 1/8 inch –thick rounds

Directions

Rinse and drain the shrimp, and set aside.

In a medium sized bowl, mix the dill weed, onion, paprika, and lemon juice.

Fold the shrimp into the mixture.

Serve the shrimp on the lettuce strips

Top with hard-boiled egg slices.

Tuna Salad

Ingredients

1 medium can albacore tuna, packed in water

2 small jars diced pimentos

½ red onion, chopped

½ cup celery, chopped

1 teaspoon paprika

1 teaspoon freshly squeezed lemon juice

½ cup low fat or homemade mayonnaise

1 cup romaine lettuce, shredded

1 tablespoon flaxseed oil

½ teaspoon freshly ground pepper to taste

Directions

Drain the tuna and then place in a colander. Rinse thoroughly to remove any salt.

In a bowl, combine the tuna with onion, celery, pimentos, and mayonnaise, and then mix thoroughly.

Toss the lettuce with the lemon juice and flaxseed oil.

In a medium sized serving bowl, make a bed of lettuce for the tuna mix.

Spoon the tuna mixture on the lettuce bed.

Sprinkle the salad with pepper and paprika to taste.

Shrimp and Pineapple Skewers

Ingredients

2 pounds medium sized shrimp with the shells removed

8 ounces fresh pineapple, cubed

1 tablespoon olive oil

1 tablespoon flaxseed oil

1 tablespoon lime juice

1 tablespoon fresh cilantro, minced

1 teaspoon chili powder

Wooden skewers for serving

Directions

Start the grill to medium heat, or preheat an oven to broil setting.

Thread the shrimp and pineapple chunks evenly onto the skewers.

In a small bowl, combine the olive oil with the lime juice, cilantro, and chili powder.

Drizzle the olive oil mixture over skewers.

Cook for about 6-8 minutes, turning once.

Remove the skewers from heat and drizzle them with flaxseed oil.

Deluxe Salmon Salad

Ingredients

12 ounces fresh pink salmon

2 cups lettuce leaves, shredded

1/2 cup celery, finely chopped

3/4 teaspoon freshly squeezed lemon juice

3/4 teaspoon dried basil

3/4 teaspoon coarse sea salt

1/2 cup green onions, finely chopped

1/2 cup low-fat mayonnaise

1 tablespoon avocado oil

1 tablespoon extra virgin olive oil

Directions

Place the salmon, lettuce, and celery in a medium bowl.

In a blender, combine the mayonnaise, lemon juice, egg, and mustard, and blend until frothy.

Add the avocado and olive oil into the blender, drop by drop, until you get a smooth and creamy texture

Season the mix with salt and pepper.

Place the mayonnaise mix in a sealed container and refrigerate for about 15 minutes.

Stir the prepared mayonnaise together with the remaining ingredients (except the green onions) in a medium bowl, and then toss the salad.

Sprinkle on the green onions, and then chill and serve.

Salmon And Halibut Recipes

Salmon is well represented in this cookbook because of its health benefits and versatility as a recipe ingredient. The many varieties of salmon are widely available all over the country. Fresh salmon can be frozen without losing its nutritional value, making it ideal for storage. It is widely prepared as a main dish but can also be used as a tasty ingredient in salads, soups, and appetizers. There are even ways of making "salmon jerky" - a healthful in-between-meal snack.

Because it is rich with Omega-3 oils, salmon makes for a very healthy protein option.
Being a fatty fish, salmon can be forgiving as a cooking ingredient. Aside from being mildly flavored, the oil content gives more allowance for "overcooking," unlike most other fish varieties. Salmon can be eaten raw, broiled, baked, fried, grilled, poached, and even smoked, providing many alternatives for both the rookie and seasoned chef. Salmon's saltwater counterpart, halibut, is also a mildly flavored, versatile fish. Halibut can be used as a main dish with different methods of preparation available.

Whole Poached Salmon

Ingredients

1 6-8 lb. salmon

1 onion, sliced

1 large carrot, sliced

2 bay leaves

4 sprigs parsley

1 tablespoon sea salt

Lettuce, cucumber slices, tomato wedges, and lemon twists for garnishing.

Directions

Half-fill a deep cooking pan with water. Add the onions, carrot, herbs and sea salt.

Bring to a boil and simmer for 30 minutes.

Use two long strips of muslin or aluminum foil wrapped around the salmon. While holding both ends, lower the salmon into the pan, curving it to fit.

Cover the pan and simmer gently, making sure that the water does not boil.

Simmer for around 8 minutes per pound.

To serve hot, drain the fish and serve with Hollandaise sauce or mayonnaise, salad, and new potatoes.

To serve cold, leave fish to cool in the liquid.

Arrange the fish on a large serving dish and garnish with lemon twists, cucumber slices of cucumber and a lettuce and tomato salad.

Serve with a side of mayonnaise. The skin can also be removed before garnishing.

Dill And Caper Salmon Burgers

<u>Ingredients</u>

1½ - 2 pounds of skinless and boneless wild salmon

2 teaspoons mustard

2 tablespoons dill, finely chopped

1 tablespoon capers

1 jalapeño pepper, pitted, finely chopped

2 tablespoons red onion, finely chopped

¼ teaspoon sea salt

1 lemon, cut into wedges for garnish

<u>Directions</u>

Cut the salmon into chunks and place ¼ of it in a food processor with the mustard.

Put on pulse setting until the salmon forms into a smooth paste. This paste-like texture will help hold the burgers together.

Add the remaining salmon and ingredients in the blender and put on pulse setting only enough to break the salmon up into small chunks. Be careful not to blend so that the remaining salmon becomes smooth.

Shape the salmon into burgers.

The formed burgers can be pan fried with a little oil or grilled.

Cook the burgers for 3-5 minutes until firm and easy to flip.

Continue cooking the second side for another 3-5 minutes.

Serve with lemon wedges.

Halibut In Butter Sauce

Ingredients

1 pound halibut, sliced about 1-inch thick

6 tablespoons butter

1 shallot, finely chopped

½ cup cooking, or dry white wine

½ cup chicken stock

1 tablespoon parsley, finely chopped

1 lemon, cut into wedges

Directions

Pat the halibut dry and lightly season with salt and pepper.

In medium heat, place 1 tablespoon of the butter in a skillet and add the halibut.

After about 2 minutes when the butter begins to brown, add another tablespoon of butter and the shallots.

Turn up the heat slightly and add the wine, simmering rapidly for three minutes.

Add the chicken stock and continue simmering the mixture for about 5 more minutes, spooning some of the broth over the halibut.

Reduce cooker to medium-low heat, and stir in the parsley.

Add the remaining butter slowly, in small chunks.

Cover the skillet and let simmer for 4-6 minutes until the halibut is cooked through and flakes apart easily with a fork.

Serve with the lemon wedges.

Halibut Tacos with Citrus Dressing

Ingredients

2 pounds of halibut

2 tablespoons of lemon pepper seasoning powder

1 teaspoon olive oil

1 red onion, sliced thinly

Lettuce leaves

Thinly sliced cabbage

For the citrus dressing

1 cup low fat or homemade mayonnaise

4 small limes

2 garlic cloves, finely chopped

Directions

Season the fish with lemon pepper and drizzle olive oil on top.

Pan-fry, grill, or broil the halibut. This should only take about 4 minutes per side for the halibut to be fully cooked.

While the halibut is cooking, grate the green peel from the limes to make zest.

Cut the limes open to squeeze out the juice.

In a small bowl, mix the mayonnaise, garlic and lime zest.

Slowly add the lime juice until. Test for flavor and consistency occasionally to make sure the dressing is to your taste.

Curry Salmon

Ingredients

2 8-oz. salmon steaks

2 tablespoons lemon pepper seasoning powder

2 teaspoons curry powder

1 teaspoons turmeric

1 cup salt-free chicken stock

4 teaspoons cooking or white wine

Directions

Wash the salmon, and place it in shallow baking dish.

Mix the curry, pepper, and turmeric with the chicken stock, and pour over fish.

Pour in the wine, and cover the dish with foil.

Bake at 350 F for 20-30 minutes. Salmon should flake easily with fork.

Baked Salmon

Ingredients

2 8-ounce salmon steaks

2 tablespoons lemon pepper seasoning powder

4 tablespoons lemon juice

1 teaspoon dill weed

2 tablespoon finely chopped fresh chives

1 lime, cut into wedges

Directions

Place each salmon steak on a piece of aluminum foil large enough to wrap it.

Pour the lemon juice over each steak, and sprinkle with dill.

Seal each steak in an aluminum foil pouch.

Place the aluminum-sealed steaks in a Pyrex dish and bake at 350 F for 30 minutes, or until the salmon flakes easily with a fork.

Serve salmon sprinkled with chives and lime wedges.

Spicy Salmon Steaks

Ingredients

4 salmon steaks, total of about 1¾-2 lb.

For the Marinade mix

2 tablespoons light soy sauce

1 tablespoon extra-virgin olive oil

1 teaspoon garlic, chopped

1 teaspoon ginger, chopped

1 teaspoon Chinese, five-spice powder

1 tablespoon coriander, chopped

Directions

Place the salmon in a shallow dish for marinating.

Mix the ingredients for the marinade, and pour the mixture over the salmon and marinate for 2 hours.

Remove the salmon steaks from the marinade and cook on a preheated griddle or grill for about 4-5 minutes on each side, basting the steaks with the marinade.

Tropical Coconut Salmon

Ingredients

2 lb. fresh salmon fillet

¼ cup organic sugar

1½ tablespoons cornstarch

½ cup extra virgin coconut oil

1 cup organic mango juice

2 tablespoons organic soy sauce

1–1½ cups coconut chips

Extra coconut oil to grease the pan

Directions

Preheat oven to 375 F.

Place the salmon in a roasting pan greased with coconut oil.

Arrange coconut chips over salmon.

Mix the sugar and cornstarch in a small bowl.

In a small saucepan, melt the coconut oil over low heat.

While it melts, add the mango juice and soy sauce to the coconut oil.

Add the sugar mixture while stirring constantly.

Continue stirring until the mango sauce starts to thicken. When this happens, remove the sauce quickly from heat.

Pour the mango sauce over the salmon.

Bake the salmon for about fifteen minutes.

Check if the salmon is done by gently pulling at the fish a few inches from its edge. The salmon is done once it is flaky and lighter in color.

Poached Halibut

Ingredients

4 halibut fillets, 4-6 ounces each

2 lemons, 1 sliced into rounds and 1 cut into wedges

2 tablespoons flaxseed oil, cold-pressed

1 tablespoon fresh dill

1 tablespoon freshly ground black pepper

1 tablespoon garlic powder

4 lemons, cut into wedges

Directions

Insert a steamer basket into a four-quart pan and fill it with 1 inch of water.

Place the lemon slices in a basket and bring to a boil.

Layer the pan with the halibut, reduce heat to low, let it simmer for ten minutes, and then remove from pan.

After removing, drizzle the halibut with the flaxseed oil, followed by the pepper, garlic powder, and dill.

Garnish with lemon wedges.

Nectarine Salmon Fillet

Ingredients

2 tablespoons of minced fresh cilantro

2 tablespoons of minced red onion

2 tablespoons of lime juice, freshly squeezed

4 salmon fillets

2 tablespoons olive oil, extra virgin variety

1 nectarine, large, to be cut into thin wedges

Directions

Preheat oven to 425 F.

In a small bowl, mix onion, cilantro, and lime juice.
Brush the skin side of the fillet with a tablespoon of
olive oil.

Place fillets on a wire rack, skin side down.

Press the nectarine wedges onto the salmon flesh and then cover abundantly with lime mixture.

Drizzle with what's left of the olive oil. Bake for 15 minutes.

Salmon Caesar Salad

Ingredients

2 heads of romaine lettuce, chopped

4 6-ounce salmon fillets with skin

2 tablespoons of olive oil, extra virgin variety

2 tablespoons of flaxseed oil, cold-pressed

¼ of a small onion, red, diced

1 clove of garlic, crushed

1 teaspoon of mustard seed, crushed

1 tablespoon of lemon juice, freshly squeezed

Black pepper, freshly ground

Directions

Preheat oven with heat settings appropriate for broiling.

Brush the flesh side of the fillet with a tablespoon of olive oil. Then, place salmon fillets in a baking pan with the fish facing flesh side down.

Using the remaining tablespoon of olive oil, brush the skin. Broil fillet for 15 minutes.

Remove from oven. Set aside.

Combine lettuce and onion in a large bowl.

In a small jar, mix garlic, flaxseed oil, lemon juice, and mustard seed. Shake well and then toss with the lettuce and onion mixture.

Serve salad with salmon fillet as toppings, and season with black pepper to taste.

Halibut in Lemon Cream

Ingredients

4 halibut fillets, cut into serving pieces (6 oz. each) and wiped with a damp cloth

Salt

Heavy cream

Grated onion

Freshly grated lemon peel

Fresh lemon juice

Freshly ground black pepper (optional)

Thin lemon slices

Directions

Sprinkle the fish pieces lightly with salt. Arrange them in a single layer in a shallow, buttered baking dish.

Combine the cream, onion, lemon peel, lemon juice and 1/2 teaspoon of salt, and pour over the fish.

Bake, uncovered, in a preheated 400-degree oven for 20 minutes.

Spoon the cream sauce over the fish as you serve it.

Grind on black pepper, if desired.

Garnish with the lemon slices.

Broiled Salmon

Ingredients

Salmon fillets, with the skin left on

Butter

Salt

Freshly ground black pepper

Lemon wedges

Directions

Melt the butter in a shallow, fireproof dish large enough to hold the fillets in one layer.

Dry the fillets and lay them in the dish, turning them to coat both sides with butter.

Cook the fish, skin side down, 4 inches from the heat in a broiler preheated to its highest setting. Baste occasionally with the butter. Do not turn the fillets.

Cook 6-8 minutes, until the flesh is opaque and flakes when prodded with a fork.

Sprinkle with salt and a few grindings of pepper

Surround the fillets with lemon wedges and serve in the dish.

Halibut Teriyaki

Ingredients

6 fish fillets (about 2 lb. in total)

1/3 cup Soy sauce

1/3 cup Mirin

1/3 cup Sake

Garlic clove, finely chopped (optional)

Directions

Mix the soy sauce, mirin and sake together in a small saucepan and bring to a boil.

Add the garlic, if using.

Remove the pan from the stove, pour the soy-sauce mixture over the fish fillets and marinate them for 15 to 20 minutes.

Preheat the broiler or charcoal grill, and cook the pieces 4 inches from the heat for 5 to 10 minutes on each side, brushing them three or four times with the marinade.

When finished, the fish should be coated with a rich brown glaze.

Serve immediately.

Salmon Roe and Cucumber Rounds

Ingredients

2 ounces salmon roe

1-2 cucumbers, sliced into rounds

1 avocado, cut into small chunks

1 sheet of seafood nori, cut into small squares

Directions

Lay cucumber rounds on serving platter.

Set a square of nori on each cucumber slice and top with avocado and salmon roe.

Salmon with Tomatoes and Mushroom

Ingredients

2 4-6 oz. salmon fillets

1 tablespoon of olive oil, extra virgin variety

1 teaspoon of round paprika

1 teaspoon of fresh dill, finely chopped

½ teaspoon freshly ground black pepper

1 red tomato, large diced

4 ounces of white mushrooms, sliced

Directions

Prepare a large saucepan with a steamer basket and 1 inch water.

Bring to a boil. Reduce heat to simmer, place salmon in steamer, and cook for fifteen minutes.

Heat oil in a cast iron skillet over medium flame.

Add mushrooms, paprika, dill and pepper, and then sauté for five minutes.

Add then tomato and keep cooking for five more minutes. Remove skillet from heat.

Once the fillets are cooked, remove them from then pan.

To serve, top with tomato-mushroom mixture.

Tuna, Cod, And Game Fish Recipes

Tuna and cod are saltwater fish that are popular as main entrees. Tuna flesh is tender, flaky, and, like salmon and halibut, flavorful. Tuna is sold fresh or frozen and available as fillets and steaks, which makes it ideal for healthy grilling. Tuna can also be cooked by broiling or baking. It is a popular fish in raw seafood circles. It is also the most popular canned fish variety, packed in either water or oil.

The other fish in this section, such as snapper, swordfish, haddock, and mackerel, are also easily obtainable year round and can also be purchased fresh or frozen.

Coconut Citrus Tuna Steaks

Ingredients

Extra virgin olive oil

1½ tablespoons coconut butter, softened

Any seafood-seasoning blend

1½ tablespoons lime juice, freshly squeezed

2 medium-sized tuna steaks, thawed

Extra virgin coconut oil

Directions

Rub olive oil and seasoning on both sides of the tuna steaks. Combine equal parts of coconut butter and lime juice. Beat moisture using a fork until consistency is smooth and creamy.

Thickly coat both sides of the tuna steak with the coconut mixture. Allow coating to harden (this will only for a few seconds) and flip the steak to coat the other side. Marinate for 10 minutes.

Grease frying pan or skillet coated using extra virgin coconut oil, and then preheat over medium heat settings for 5 minutes.

Cook steaks until desired doneness is achieved. Cooking time will vary depending on the thickness of the steaks (the rule of thumb is 2-3 minutes per side results to medium-rare doneness for tuna steak). Be careful when flipping steaks to retain coating.

Serve immediately with rice and green vegetables.

Baked Cod

Ingredients

1 lb. of cod filets

½ cup cooking or white wine

¼ yellow onion, sliced

2 tablespoons freshly-squeezed lemon juice

1 tablespoon dried dill

1 teaspoon turmeric

Directions

Wash the cod well in cool water, then place the fish in a shallow baking dish. Pour in the wine.

Spread the onion slices evenly over the fish.

Sprinkle the fish with the lemon juice, dill, and turmeric.

Cover the dish with aluminum foil, and bake at 375 F for about 20 minutes, or until the fish flakes easily with a fork.

Breakfast Tuna Sashimi

WARNING: Please be careful when purchasing the tuna for this recipe (check for freshness).

Ingredients

2 tablespoons coconut oil

2 cups spinach, torn into bite-sized pieces

2 pieces ahi tuna sashimi, 4-6 ounces each, thinly sliced

1 cup mango or peach slices

½ cup blueberries

Directions

Warm the coconut oil over low flame until liquid. Combine with spinach and toss well.

Arrange sashimi over spinach with mango or peach slices, and scatter with berries.

Grilled Tuna Steaks

Ingredients

4 (2-inch-thick) tuna steaks, about 8 ounces each

3 tablespoons sesame oil

Sea salt, or Kosher salt

Freshly cracked black pepper to taste

¼ cup white pepper, freshly cracked

Directions

Build a two-level fire on the grill (this means placing all the coals on one side of the grill and leaving the other side of the grill free of coals).

When the flames have died down, meaning that all the coals are covered with gray ash, and the temperature is hot you're ready to cook. You can easily check the grill temperature by holding your hand about 6 inches over the coals for about 2 to 3 seconds.

Rub sesame oil all over the tuna steaks and sprinkle the steaks generously with the salt and peppers.

Pat gently to make sure that the peppers and salt stick to the tuna.

Place the tuna steaks slowly on the grill and directly over the coals and grill them until well seared on both sides or done in the way you like them.

It will take about 4 to 5 minutes total for a medium rare tuna, and 6 to 8 minutes for the tuna to be cooked all the way through.

You can check for doneness by cutting into one of the pieces of tuna to see if it is done in the way you want it to be when you eat it. Remember that fish, like meat, will continue to cook a little bit after it is removed from the grill.

Remove the tuna steaks from the grill and serve warm.

Spicy Coconut Fish

Ingredients

1 lb. fresh fish fillets (rozen fish will do just as well)

2 tablespoons virgin coconut oil

Cayenne pepper to taste

Salt to taste

1 onion, diced

2 cloves garlic, minced

2 tablespoons coconut butter

2 cups water

Directions

Defrost frozen fillets.

Heat the coconut oil in a frying pan. Season the fish
fillets and fry until lightly brown.

Remove the fillets, and add onion, garlic, coconut butter, and water to the pan.

Bring to boil for around 10 minutes, or until mixture thickens slightly.

Return the fish fillets to the pan with the coconut cream mixture.

Cover the pan and cook the fish for an additional 5 minutes.

Serve with rice, fresh salad, or steamed vegetables.

Cajun Catfish Bake

Ingredients

2 lb. catfish, thoroughly washed

4 tablespoons extra-virgin olive oil

1 clove garlic, minced

3 tablespoons lemon juice

1 ½ teaspoon black pepper

½ teaspoon cayenne pepper

½ teaspoon turmeric

Directions

Place the catfish into a 9 × 13-inch baking dish, greased with a little olive oil.

Heat the rest of the olive oil in a saucepan, and then sauté garlic.

Pour the olive oil sauté over catfish.

Sprinkle the fish with lemon juice and sprinkle the remaining spices evenly.

Bake at 350 F for 25 to 30 minutes.

Grilled Snapper

Ingredients

4 red snapper fillets, around 4-6 ounces each

½ teaspoon oregano

½ teaspoon turmeric

½ teaspoon paprika

½ teaspoon white pepper

2 tablespoons extra virgin olive oil

Directions

Set grill to medium heat, or preheat an oven to broil setting.

Combine the paprika, oregano, white pepper, and turmeric into a small bowl.

Brush the olive oil onto fillets and coat these evenly with the spice mixture.

Grill or broil for around 8 minutes, turning them at the halfway point.

Peruvian Style Picante Mackerel

Ingredients

One whole mackerel (2 lb.), or several small fish, cleaned and cut into serving pieces

Coarse sea salt

1 garlic clove, crushed

Yellow or green pepper, pitted, and chopped

Fresh bitter orange juice

Directions

Cover the fish on all sides with a thick coat of coarse sea salt and let stand for at least 1 hour.

Place the orange juice, garlic, and pepper into a saucepan and pour in just enough water to cover the top of the fish. Bring the mixture to the boiling point.

Wash away the salt from the pieces of fish and gently place the fish on the pan.

Bring it rapidly back to the boiling point and cover tightly.

Serve immediately with white rice or steamed vegetables.

New England Baked Fish

Ingredients

Whole bluefish (around 3 lb.) cleaned

Salt and pepper

Paprika

Freshly squeezed lemon juice

Melted butter

Directions

Rub the bluefish with the salt, pepper and paprika. Place the fish into a buttered baking dish.

Slowly pour equal parts of lemon juice and melted butter on the fish.

Cover the fish with buttered brown paper and bake in a preheated 350 F oven for 30 minutes.

Serve with the sauce.

Sweet and Savory Swordfish

Ingredients

4 6-ounce swordfish steaks

4 garlic cloves, minced

2 tablespoons olive oil

2 tablespoons unpeeled ginger root, minced

Freshly-squeezed juice from 1 lime

2 teaspoons chili powder

Directions

Preheat oven to broil setting.

Combine the oil, lime juice, ginger, garlic, and chili powder into a small bowl and mix well.

Evenly coat the surface of a 9 x 13-inch baking dish with half of the ginger mixture. Add fish and cover it with the remaining ginger mixture.

Place the dish in the oven and broil for 15 minutes, turning it at the halfway point.

Baked Haddock Italian Style

<u>Ingredients</u>

2 lb. haddock, fresh or frozen

6 tablespoons extra virgin olive oil

6 tablespoons fresh parsley, chopped

4 tomatoes, diced

3 cloves garlic, minced

1 red onion, minced

1 green pepper, chopped

1 teaspoon dried basil

1 teaspoon dill weed

1/4 teaspoon black pepper

2 tablespoons freshly-squeezed lemon juice

<u>Directions</u>

Thoroughly wash fresh haddock in cool water and set aside.

Heat the olive oil in a heavy skillet, and sauté the garlic and onion until tender.

Add the green peppers and continue sautéing on low heat until tender.

Add the tomatoes, black pepper, parsley, basil, and dill.

Remove the sautéed pepper mix from the heat and spread half of the sauce on the inside of a 9 × 13-inch baking dish.

Place fish on top, and pour any remaining sauce over entire fish.

Sprinkle with lemon juice.

Cover the dish with foil, and bake at 375 F for 15 to 20 minutes, or until flaky (check gently with a fork).

Tuna Sailor-Style

Ingredients

2 lb. tuna steaks of about 6-8 ounces each

1/3 cup onion, chopped

2 tbsp. olive oil

3-1/2 cups canned whole tomatoes, do not drain

1 teaspoon sea salt.

1/4 teaspoon black pepper

1 teaspoon dried basil herb

1/3 cup capers, rinsed and drained

Directions

In a large skillet, sauté the onions in hot olive oil for 3 minutes.

Stir in the tomatoes, capers, basil, salt and pepper.

Cover the pan and simmer the tomato mixture for 15 minutes, seasoning to taste.

Place the tuna steaks in the sauce and poach these until the fish flakes at the touch of a fork and looks opaque. Cook for about 5 minutes on each side.

Place the tuna on a platter and spoon the remaining sauce over it.

Red Snapper in Zesty Sauce

Ingredients

2 lbs. red snapper filets

¼ cup extra virgin olive oil

2 cloves garlic

2 tablespoons freshly squeezed lemon juice

½ cup freshly squeezed lime juice

4 scallions, sliced thin

2 tomatoes, diced

1 teaspoon cayenne pepper

1 teaspoon black pepper

½ green bell pepper, chopped

½ red bell pepper, chopped

Cilantro to taste

Directions

Heat the olive oil in a skillet, and sauté the garlic until golden brown.

Lay the fish in oil, and sprinkle with the lime and lemon juice.

Sprinkle cayenne and black peppers over the dish, and then add the tomatoes, scallions, and red and green bell peppers.

Cover and simmer for 15 minutes, or until fish flakes easily with a fork.

Add cilantro garnish.

Roasted Swordfish with Mushrooms

Ingredients

4 swordfish steaks, about 4-6 ounces each

2 tablespoons olive oil

1 cup mixed wild mushrooms

1 medium shallot, minced

1 tablespoon fresh parsley, minced

2 garlic cloves, minced

¼ cup cooking, or dry white wine

Directions

Preheat oven to 425 F.

Heat 1 tablespoon of the olive oil in a heavy or cast iron skillet over a medium flame.

Add the mushrooms and cook for five minutes.

Add the shallots and cook for another. Add the garlic and stir for 30 seconds.

Stir in the parsley and wine and bring the mixture to a boil.

Scrape the browned bits from the surface of skillet and mix in with the liquid.

Remove the mixture from the heat.

Nudge the mushroom mixture to sides of skillet, making room for the swordfish in the center.

Place the swordfish in the skillet and drizzle it with the remaining tablespoon of olive oil.

Pour on the mushroom mix and cover the fish, baking it for 15 minutes.

Baked Tuna

Ingredients

4 tuna steaks (1 inch thick)

½ cup unsalted butter, melted

1/2 teaspoon sea salt

2 teaspoons fresh dill, finely cut

1 lemon, cut into wedges

Directions

Preheat the oven to 450 F.

Brush a shallow baking dish lightly with ½ teaspoon of the melted butter. Place the tuna steaks on it.

Mix the sea salt with the remaining butter and brush some of the mixture lightly over the tops of the fish.

Bake the steaks in the oven for 10-12 minutes.

Remove the steaks from the oven, and set a broiler to the highest setting.

Brush the steaks with butter, and then place them under the broiler until brown.

Turn the steaks gently without piercing.

After turning the steaks, brush them with the rest of the butter and broil for another 2 minutes.

Sprinkle the steaks with the dill and serve with the lemon wedges

Add steamed vegetables or rice as a side dish.

Cod with Lemon Dressing

Ingredients

1 pound fresh or frozen cod

2 tablespoons sesame oil

2 garlic cloves, finely chopped

3 tablespoons freshly-squeezed lemon juice

3 scallions, chopped

Directions

Put several cups of water on boil, and preheat an oven broiler to high.

Pat the cod fillets dry then drizzle lightly with the salt and pepper.

Cover the fillets with 2 tablespoons of sesame oil and the garlic and broil for about 10 minutes.

Check if the cod is done cooking by piercing it with a fork. The cod will flake apart easily when done.

Mix the remaining sesame oil with lemon juice.

Cover the cod with the mixture.

Baked Trout

Ingredients

2 rainbow or other trout, 10-12 inches long, each

2 tablespoons oil

½ yellow onion, diced

2 tablespoons Chardonnay or cooking wine

1 teaspoon fresh dill, minced

1 teaspoon paprika

Freshly squeezed juice from half a lemon

Directions

Clean the trout thoroughly. Place them on an aluminum foil sheet large enough to wrap entire fish.

Preheat an oven to 350 F.

In a small cast iron skillet, heat the oil over a medium flame. Add the onion and sauté for 5 minutes until tender.

Remove the onions from the pan and place it in a small mixing bowl.

Mix the onions with wine, dill, paprika, and the lemon juice.

Stuff the trout with the onion mixture. Wrap it securely with foil and bake for 20 minutes.

Salt Baked Snapper

Ingredients

2 lb. whole snapper, gutted, rinsed, and patted dry

4 lb. sea salt or kosher salt, add more as needed

2 lb. whole snapper (lane snapper is preferred) or other variety of firm fish, rinsed, gutted, and patted dry

Ground black pepper

2 sprigs rosemary, fresh

Directions

Preheat the oven to 400 F.

On a large (about 9 x 13") baking sheet make a bed of salt about one inch deep. Lay the fish in the middle of the salt bed.

Sprinkle black pepper into the interior of the fish.

Stuff in the rosemary sprigs.

Pour the sea salt over top to cover to form a solid and think mound over on fish, covering all visible skin.

Place the fish in the oven and bake for 40 minutes.

With an oven thermometer, check the fish's internal temperature with an instant-read thermometer.

Ensure that it has reached at least 137 F before removing the pan from the oven.

Crack open and peel off the salt crust and fish skin with a knife and fork. If the skin use the fork and knife to remove the skin, if needed.

Baked Cod Nuggets

This can be prepared in advance and kept in the freezer for a healthy meal you want available in a snap.

Ingredients

1/2 lb. cod fillets

2 tablespoons lemon juice

1 organic or Omega-3 egg

2 tablespoons Dijon mustard

2 tablespoons unflavored yogurt

Salt and pepper to taste

Breadcrumbs

3 tablespoons milk

Directions

Preheat the oven to 350 F. Line a large baking tray with baking parchment.

Mix the milk, egg, yogurt, and mustard in a bowl.

Cut fish fillet into bite-sized pieces and drizzle the lemon juice with a spoon.

Add the salt and pepper to taste.

Dip the fish nuggets into yogurt and milk sauce and cover the nuggets with the mixture.

Remove the nuggets from the sauce with a fork and allow the excess sauce drip off.

Coat the nuggets with the breadcrumbs.

Place the fillet nuggets on the baking tray and bake for 10 minutes. Broil until golden brown.

Serve hot with your choice of sauce or dip.

Shrimp, Crab, Squid, And Shellfish Recipes

Shrimp is a versatile type of seafood. Many varieties of all sizes can be purchased anywhere, either fresh or frozen. Shrimp has very little visible fat (typically 1%) and can be cooked with practically no sauces or garnishing. Additionally, it is a popular choice for omelets, appetizers, and salads to augment a pesecetarian meal.

Crab and shellfish are tasty additions as entrees and appetizers. Crabmeat is increasingly being made available in canned and frozen varieties. There is a variety of Alaskan Pollock called "surimi," which is packaged as "imitation" crabmeat. This is less expensive than real crabmeat and has higher carbohydrate content.

Shrimp Stuffed With Avocados

<u>Ingredients</u>

1-½ cup bay shrimp or small salad shrimp, peeled, cooked and washed

4 large avocados, with the seeds removed, peeled and halved

1 tablespoon paprika

1 tablespoon onion powder

1 teaspoon black pepper

1 tablespoon lemon juice

<u>Directions</u>

Place avocados on a serving plate with cut sides facing up.

In a mixing bowl, combine the shrimp, onion powder, lemon juice, and pepper.

Spoon the shrimp mixture onto each avocado half, covering generously.

Sprinkle the top of each shrimp-stuffed avocado with paprika before serving.

Barbecued Alaskan Shrimp

Ingredients

2-½ lb. shelled and steamed jumbo shrimp with tails left on

¼ cup olive oil

2 tablespoons lemon juice

3 garlic cloves, minced

1/8 teaspoon paprika

Pinch of cayenne pepper

3 fresh limes, cut into wedges

4 sprigs fresh parsley

Directions

Place cooked shrimp in a large bowl.

Mix olive oil, garlic, spices, and lemon juice in a separate bowl.

Brush shrimp with spice mixture.

Place the shrimp on a hot grill or under a broiler for 1-2 minutes.

Turn the shrimp and continue cooking them for an additional 1-2 minutes.

Garnish the dish with lime wedges.

Add parsley on the top of the dish.

Shrimp Delight

Ingredients

2 lb. jumbo shrimp, head on unpeeled

1 tablespoon lime juice

2 tablespoons olive oil

1 garlic clove, minced

4 seeded plum tomatoes, sliced into very thin wedges

½ cup shredded basil

1 lime, cut into quarters

Directions

Using large scissors or kitchen shears, cut a thin slice down the backs of each of the shrimp, while leaving the peel on.

Snip shrimp legs with the scissors.

In a large mixing bowl, tss the shrimp gently with lime juice. Set aside.

Heat the olive oil in a cast iron skillet over a medium flame.

Add the garlic and cook for thirty seconds.

Layer the skillet with shrimp and cook for 2 minutes, turning once.

Add the tomatoes and cook for about 2 minutes, stirring about after a minute.

Garnish the dish with the basil and lime quarters

Steamed Mussels

Ingredients

1 lb. fresh mussels in shells

½ cup water

2 tablespoon olive oil

1 clove garlic, minced

1 teaspoon dill

1 tablespoon fresh squeezed lemon juice

½ cup cooking wine or dry white wine

Directions

Steam mussels in water until the shells open.

While the mussels are steaming, sauté the garlic in olive oil.

Add wine, lemon juice, and dill, lemon.

Let simmer for about three minutes.

When mussels open up, put these on a large serving plate and pour the mixture over each.

Crab Dip

This can be used for raw vegetable slices such as carrots, celery, or cucumber.

Ingredients

½ pound crab meat

1 teaspoon tomato paste

¼ cup fresh or low fat mayonnaise

1 tablespoon chopped chives

1 teaspoon horseradish

1 teaspoon lemon juice

Tabasco or other hot sauce to taste

Directions

Whisk together the mayonnaise, tomato paste, lemon juice, mayonnaise, chives, horseradish and hot sauce.

Stir in the crabmeat.

Serve with the raw vegetables.

Lime and Dill Crab

Ingredients

2 large cooked Dungeness crabs, cracked, shelled, and chilled

3 tablespoons lime juice

2 teaspoon paprika

2 teaspoon dried, ground dill weed

3 limes, cut into wedges

4 sprigs parsley, finely chopped

Directions

Drizzle the crabmeat pieces with lime juice, and sprinkle with paprika and dill.

Garnish with lime wedges and parsley.

Squid with Tomato and Basil

Ingredients

2 large tomatoes, cut into slices or wedges

1 cup fresh basil, roughly chopped

4 tablespoons olive oil

1 pound cleaned squid, bodies and tentacles

3 garlic cloves, finely chopped

1 teaspoon salt

Directions

Heat a grill to high or preheat an oven broiler to high.

Combine tomatoes and basil on a platter. Drizzle with 2 tablespoons of olive oil.

Rinse squid and pat dry.

Toss with garlic, salt, and remaining 2 tablespoons of olive oil.

If grilling, thread squid on skewers, separating bodies and tentacles on different skewers.*

If cooking under the broiler, simply put squid in a pan.

Cook squid until it firms up, about 5-7 minutes.

Toss squid with tomatoes and basil. Add additional salt and olive oil to taste.

Broiled Lobster Tail

<u>Ingredients</u>

4 small fresh lobster tails

1 lemon, ½ juiced, ½ cut into 4 wedges

2 tablespoons minced fresh parsley

Freshly ground black pepper, to taste

<u>Directions</u>

Preheat oven to broil.

With a sharp knife, slice vertically down the backs of the lobster tails and pull them slightly apart. Sprinkle with lemon juice, parsley, and pepper.

Broil for 8-10 minutes until the meat is opaque. Garnish with lemon wedges.

Oyster Shooters

Ingredients

2 shucked oysters

Dash of freshly ground black pepper

1 teaspoon freshly squeezed lemon juice, divided

6 tablespoons vodka, divided

1 tablespoon tomato juice, divided

1 tablespoon hot sauce, divided

Directions

Season the oysters with pepper. Place each oyster in a 3-ounce shooter or cordial glass.

Add a half-teaspoon of lemon juice to each glass, and then pour 3 tablespoons vodka over each oyster.

To finish, add equal amounts of tomato juice and hot sauce to the shooters. Bottoms up!

Peach and Ginger Scallops

Ingredients

1 shallot, large, minced

2 tablespoons olive oil, extra virgin variety

1 tablespoon ginger root, freshly grated

2 large peaches, peeled, cored, and coarsely chopped

2 lb. sea scallops

Juice from half a lime

Directions

Grease a cast iron skillet with a tablespoon of oil. Preheat over medium flame.

Add the shallot and then cook for 2 minutes. Add in ginger and then stir for about half a minute.

Add in peaches. Continue cooking for 3 minutes, stirring the mixture at the halfway point. Transfer the peach mixture into a small bowl. Cover bowl to keep peaches warm.

Add what's left of the olive oil into the pan and then place the scallops in a single layer.

Cook for 4 to 6 minutes, turning the scallops only once.

Return the peach mixture into the skillet, making sure to cover shallots evenly.

Immediately remove from heat. Drizzle lime juice over the peaches and scallops.

Scallops with Almonds and Bacon

Ingredients

4 slices of bacon

½ cup almonds

1 large handful parsley

1 tablespoon olive oil

1 tablespoon butter

1 pound scallops

Directions

Cook the bacon until crispy, and then cool slightly and crumble into a food processor with almonds and parsley. Pulse until almonds are in small pieces.

Heat the oil and butter in a large skillet over medium-high heat until the butter foam subsides.

Add the scallops to the skillet. Turn the heat to high and cook for about 2 minutes or until scallops are brown on one side, and then turn and brown the other side for another minute or two. This will leave the scallops cooked but rare in the middle. For a firmer texture, cook the scallops 1-2 minutes more.

Transfer the scallops to a plate and sprinkle with bacon nut mixture.

Conclusion

Thank you again for grabbing both of our books on the Pescetarian diet. This diet has helped so many people over the years. There is no doubt in my mind that these recipes can assist you in reaching whatever your health and fitness goals are, from weight loss to muscle gain.

I hope that you enjoyed the recipes that I have compiled for you here. I tried to make sure that there is something for every taste, budget, and occasion. The recipes are all easy to prepare, and the ingredients and cooking equipment are all readily available at your local grocery store.

I am confident that trying out these recipes will make you appreciate the simplicity, variety, and versatility of seafood and a pescetarian diet in general.

If you've enjoyed any of these recipes in particular, please take the time to share your thoughts by sending me a personal message, or even posting a review on Amazon. It would be greatly appreciated and I try my best to get back to every message!

Bon Appétit!